THE INTIMATE GRAND

Colorado River sunrise from Whites Butte

THE INTIMATE GRAND

Inside Arizona's GRAND CANYON

Text by Dowling Campbell
Photographs by Mark Jefferson

NORTHLAND PRESS
FLAGSTAFF, ARIZONA

COVER: View from Yaki Point
HALF TITLE: Looking north from Desert View

Text copyright © 1985 by Dowling Campbell
Photographs copyright © 1985 by Mark Jefferson
All Rights Reserved
FIRST EDITION
Library of Congress Catalog Card Number 84-62425
Composed and Printed in the United States of America

Special thanks to Dr. Harvey Butchart and Dr. Charles Barnes for reviewing the manuscript. Their expertise and familiarity with the canyon and its past have proved invaluable.

*Dox Castle,
Shinumo Amphitheater*

The Intimate Grand

Mammoth stone serpent for the Western world
worthy of creating and absorbing original sin,
pine whispered before shouted among the din
of the frothy Colorado River, rock whirled

raft eater, ever threatening to devour
trees or humans which dare to dare to run
the killer rapids, for profit or for fun
including those who dam for profit
and for power.

No blushing, no hoping nor regretting,
this strange mountain range in reverse—
all before man's divine or perverse
self-appointed task of unadulterated begetting.

White rimmed, red walled,
the inner gorge's pressured climb;
green fire hardened to the truth of time.

Dowling Campbell

INTRODUCTION

The intimacy of the Grand Canyon must be experienced: lush ferns dangling from an overhanging cliff; crystal pools of water nurturing deer and sheep in the morning, refreshing hiker and boater in the afternoon; miles of isolation allowing the mind to be in all time frames at once. Experience. That great teacher of life. That one abstraction that allows a person to absorb knowledge as if through osmosis.

To experience all of the Grand Canyon is, of course, impossible. It requires more than standing on Maricopa Point, Grandeur or Yavapai points, or any of the other overlooks near the Grand Canyon Village, where the viewer sees

Zoraster Temple from Yaki Point

Red leaf, Havasu Canyon

only twenty miles of canyon westward and slightly less to the east and across to the north; where, from the eastern vistas, the river is scarcely visible, glinting up in brief segments between ridges and buttes.

The geographical wonder simply cannot be seen in its entirety at any one time, or even after a thousand times. The many overlooks and view points allow glimpses of limited vistas. Hikes into the depths of the canyon provide experiences of natural intimacies where there are springs and creeks and caverns and arches and cliff dwellings; but these intimate places are tucked into nooks and crannies that defy the perspectives of the overlooks. Broader overviews will provide an appealing satellite pattern but lose intimacy altogether.

The Grand Canyon of the Colorado is a place

to experience the intimacy of nature. From its deep, living inner gorge to the sprawling rims open to seduction, the canyon offers its gifts to all who dare take them. Whether experienced physically or metaphorically, the canyon promises rewards of the grandest kind.

Since we must rely on bits and pieces of canyon intimacy—steal views from overlooks, experience trails in stretches, float the river in segments—the challenge to see and experience the Grand Canyon is a continual one. Time and effort are the costs; only the receiver may judge the rewards.

A person's respect for and understanding of the canyon is a reflection of personal goals, interests, and backgrounds. Robert Brewster Stanton understood the canyon in the typical enterprising aspect of his industrial arena, plotting in 1889 to construct a railroad through it. Stanton dared to dream of people thriving in Swiss chalets, tending sheep and goat herds on the sharp slopes, and thronging to his proposed railroad. Teddy Roosevelt perceived the canyon partially as a refuge for hunting mountain lions; hence his successful creation of the Grand Canyon Game Preserve in 1906, which protected game animals but not their predators. Joseph Wood Krutch embraced a dimension of the

Agave against Scorpion Ridge from west of Bass Canyon

Havasu Falls from above

Darwinian process in his popularization of the distinctions between the Kaibab and Abert squirrels, as well as through his evaluation of the devastating impact mountain lion hunting had on the north rim ecosystem. The canyon continues to mean many things to different people.

The canyon is a mosaic of thought and impression, of natural features and processes. The first explorers perceived it strictly in terms of conquest and fortune, both of which the rugged topography defied. Later exploiters viewed it in terms of profit—beaver pelts, minerals, tourists, a riverside railway, and hydroelectric dams. Scientists have interpreted it as an index to life, with geologists tabulating some of the earth's earliest exposed rock and zoologists cautioning about the removal of predators and encroachments into natural habitat. Photographers and artists capture concepts beyond words; hikers and river runners experience the taste, feel, and smell of the canyon in its varied moods. Experiencing is the ultimate goal—to feel and come to know the canyon, to become intimate with its secrets.

It is hoped that the following pages of prose and photography will convey these intimate experiences to those who may never secure the opportunity to enjoy them first-hand. To feel the smack of a cold wave on your face when entering a rapid, to find a trickling waterfall after hiking for hours in the hot summer sun, to spot a mule deer feeding in the dawn of a crisp, new day—all of these remind the mere human of forces much larger than we, of a time much greater than human time, of emotion that surfaces from our innermost being, of the primal, the real, the intimate.

River reflection

FROM RIVER TO RIM

Shooting a rapid. A sensual experience. Anticipation. Floating a corridor of cliffs. A roar echoes between towering rocksides. First, dull persistence, the idea of danger; then growing surges, different pitches, calls, and yelps along the inner gorge. Stomach rises and sinks with the boat. Cold sweat.

Round a bend. There it is. Foamy wavetops shake madly. Commitment. There is no turning back, no forgiveness of sins. Threshold wave is calm, yet rolls with a convulsive shrug just before dropping into a glassy chute whose power becomes evident by the boiling lip of foam under which it disappears. That lip will eat a raft, munch a kayak. An explosion sends a mushroom

Crystal Rapid

Rafts in Granite Narrows

Crystal Rapid

of water skyward twice a person's height.

In the raft, hearts beat madly. Remember all the rules. Mouth closed. Lean into the breaking waves. If tossed overboard, assume the fetal position and stay upstream of the boat. Just hang on, think positive. Suddenly the worst—or best—is over and you have survived the teasing play of the river. Now the tail waves provide a roller coaster ride, and nobody can get that grin off their faces.

Three kayaks in a row run this rapid like clockwork. One, two, three slender darts slip around the whirlpool's lip, then shoot through space, each yakker still leaning into a diligent right brace, even though their paddles suddenly grab air. A Japanese yakker was once seen to strip off the top of his wet suit on the threshold of Lava Falls, bare the rising sun printed on his t-shirt, and with a kamikaze war cry, disappear into the maelstrom.

Our third yakker had gone over in Hance Rapid. His first whitewater roll. No audience to applaud. None needed. Now he tries to cut in behind a rock so he can sit in the eddy and watch the support rafts go by. But rock eddies on the Colorado are not like eddies elsewhere. They do not appreciate the taste of kayaks. This one spits him out furiously; he paddles carefully through the tail waters, knowing they too can upset, and resolves to behave himself.

One of the support rafts is not so lucky. Rolls like a rubber donut, spilling people and everything else not tied in. An equal opportunity rapid. Everyone is pulled ashore, flushed, sputtering, laughing, even though some don't want to be. They have no other choice.

Afterglow. The rapid is run. A few sultry eddies at the bottom. Not big, like the one at Horn Creek (and many more), which can pull an unwilling raft all the way up the shoreline and give it a second ride through. Bail, then settle to a lazy flow. Look back to see those crazy waveheads still nodding. Sound as loud but no longer ominous. Don't know when to quit. Lean back on gunnel, bask in sun. Only fifty-seven more to go.

Just when you think you've seen it all, here comes the Colorado River. In earnest. Through the Grand Canyon. Up close. Roaring and frothing with a purpose. With a vengeance! The sound will hang in ears for days, in the memory for years.

Campsite in a sandy willow grove. Not too many river willows left. Many species in the willow family—arroyo, red, Gooding, coyote—unimportant to most. Crowded out by the tamarisk, brought in from the Middle East around the turn of the century. Prudes and purists like to criticize the tamarisk. It's a pretty tree, delicate, more frizzy than the willow. But the willow belongs, they say. Squatter's rights.

Plenty to do when camping on the river. Unload rafts. Get supper going. Where's the beer? Didn't lose it in the last rapid, did we? Pitch tents, or at least stake them out. Use them as ground cloths; then if it rains, flip off the sleeping bags, raise a pole or two, and scramble inside. But sleep out if possible. The sky will reward like the river. Shooting stars. An easterly satellite. If it flickers, it's an airliner. No sound in either case. There's a northbound satellite—rarer.

Sat on river bank after supper. Scary. Not because of the Sidehill Gouger or the Wampus Cat or the Wallahalla Grizzly or the Petroglyph People. It's the river. It talks, says things most

Hermit Rapid

folks ought not to hear, like, everything's okay, there is no guilt, anxiety's contrived, most of us are wrong about sin and life and death. The river deceives, invites. Nothing is good or evil but thinking makes it so. Plagiarism is one of the oldest art forms in literature. Ask Shakespeare. Turn in. Like a lover, the river will be there in the morning, like it or not.

The number of early river runners remains undetermined. There is even disagreement over who was actually the first. Could a fur trapper have slipped through the churning gorge in the 1820s? A couple of prospectors in the 1850s? How about an Indian boy in . . . whenever?

John Wesley Powell's claim to be the first through the Grand Canyon has been challenged. And not by the person who might have floated the canyon before him, but by others who caught wind of the feat.

James White, poor fellow, was merely trying to save himself from marauding Indians when he was pulled to shore in 1867 at Callville, Nevada (now under the waters of Lake Mead). He was more than half starved, nearly naked, and tethered to his makeshift raft. He told a confusing story of one prospecting partner killed by Indians on the San Juan River, the other lost in a rapid, himself being flipped off the toppling raft several times. He told of trading his revolver for the hindquarter of a dog from friendly Indians (which he promptly dropped into the river and watched "sink like a rock") and of floating for a fuzzy number of days afterwards.

Whether through the entire canyon or only the bottom portion, White's journey is a fascinating one and takes nothing away from Powell's achievement. With his right arm shot away below the elbow during the Civil War, Major Powell did what most men would not have done with two good arms. He floated the relentless river, not once but twice, and surveyed and mapped it without a water fatality—though not without a few close calls. In addition, he published a journal about the adventure.

"The waters reel and roll and boil," wrote John Wesley Powell in 1869, "and we are scarcely able to determine where we can go. Now the boat is carried to the right, perhaps close to the wall; again, she is shot into the stream, and perhaps is dragged over to the other side, where, caught in a whirlpool, she spins about. . . . The boats are entirely unmanageable; no order in their running can be preserved; now one, now another, is ahead, each crew laboring for its own preservation."

The Kolb brothers were equally remarkable in their own way. Over an extended period of years, Emery and Ellsworth performed unbelievable tasks of exploration within the Grand Canyon, the descent to Cheyeva Falls being one of the most amazing. Yet they became more famous for their river trip of 1911. The motion picture they took of this trip was the longest continually billed film in the industry. The narrative is perhaps even more remarkable; Ellsworth Kolb's book contains incident upon incident described in a low-key style that gains power as it goes.

Just one example of the Kolb's appealing personality is revealed when their younger brother Ernest desired to take the short float to the Bass Trail with them. Ellsworth writes that he and Emery had thought to present Ernest "a ride in a rapid that would be sure to give him a good ducking." The water and wind were so cold, however, that they decided to play it safe. As luck would have it, Ellsworth found trouble in smooth water, where he least expected it; the boat swamped and overturned.

None of the early river runners anticipated the trip would be popular. It was spectacular to be sure, but strenuous and dangerous. In addition to Powell, Robert B. Stanton, and the Kolbs, a list of early river running names would include the trapper George Flavell and his companion Ramon Montos; Nathaniel Galloway, who introduced the "stern first" technique; "Hum" Woolley, with two other prospectors; Russell and Monett; and Glen and Bessie Hyde.

All survived their river runs except the Hydes, who in 1928 were on their honeymoon. Running the river successfully without life jackets to the Bright Angel Creek, the Hydes visited the Kolbs, who strongly urged the couple to use life jackets for the remainder of their trip. They refused, however, and disappeared on the river. Their boat, containing Bessie's diary, was found near Diamond Creek, but the fate of the couple remains a mystery. Bessie became the first woman to float most of the Grand Canyon, even though there is some evidence that she may not have wanted to take the trip in the first place.

Hopi lore is richly connected with the Colorado River. Historian Harry C. James recounts the story of the very first person to ever run the river through the canyon, long before Powell or White or an itinerant prospector or trapper may have done it. This was a Hopi boy named Tiyo, who belonged to the Snake clan. Tiyo hollowed out a cottonwood log and began from Navajo

Mountain, which means he had many miles of smooth water before surging into the great unknown, in search of the female deity Hurung Whuti of the west.

Since these early days of floating, the Colorado River has seen the first solo run, the first rubber raft, the first commercial trip, the first power boats, both up and down the river, and the first swimmers. The river is such a popular run now that private trippers must wait up to ten years for a chance to take it.

The Colorado River churns out seventy rapids in the Grand Canyon. Changing water levels do different things to the rapids—some get bigger, some disappear altogether. Powell called this river "the great unknown." It is one of the most challenging and spectacular white-water stretches on earth. It has often been labeled the most dangerous, too.

In spite of dozens of dams now adorning the Colorado River (two of the largest at each end of Grand Canyon), an almost unmolested stretch, 250 miles of pure paradise (or hell), churns between Lake Powell and Lake Mead. The downstream thrust is absolute. Once a trip is launched, there is no turning back, no way out, except by occasional foot trail for the disheartened or by helicopter in case of injury.

Canyon vista and Colorado River from Dutton Point on Powell Plateau

Today's flood of river trippers "put in" at Lee's Ferry, Arizona. Few notice, while rafts are inflated and supplies are tied securely, a half-destroyed stone house with fortress windows on a nearby sand dune. Few realize, amidst the mud and the blazing sun, that they would have answered to the muzzle of Rachel Lee's shotgun sticking through one of the window slots had they arrived here between 1872 and 1877. Sixty-year-old John D. Lee himself would have been stationed atop a nearby stone tower called Lee's Lookout; or perhaps he would have been hiding in one of the houses on his ranch, which he called Lonely Dell. Lee would emerge only upon the assurance that the newcomers were not federal marshals but travelers interested in crossing the river. Then he would have hospitably served a sumptuous meal, including fresh vegetables, fruit, and melons grown at the ranch.

The Colorado River is an education. Reading the water requires skill and experience. Shooting a rapid demands self-control. Rowing a raft requires strength, endurance, and fitness—or at least the intelligence to make up for a lack in any of the other three.

The river is dangerous, but not as dangerous as it was before Glen Canyon Dam was built. This dam, with all its lofty concrete, power-generating capabilities, and visitor center, has brought changes to the Colorado River. One important change is the lack of silt in the water.

It was silt that gave the Colorado River the power to carve the Grand Canyon, aided by uplift. In addition to being some of the oldest rock in the world, the Vishnu Schist is also among the hardest. Thus, the river's tough assignment of cutting through granite and schist becomes even tougher without the abrasive action of silt to help. Inevitably, however, the river is destined to win its battle against rock. Although the presence of the dam has slowed the process considerably, the river's persistence is unceasing. The river's only help now comes from loose rocks that tumble and grind at the river bed.

Up until a few decades ago, one could scoop a bucket of muddy water out of the Colorado, let it sit overnight, and by morning the clear water would appear above two or three inches of silt settled at the bottom. William Guy Bass reported that Colorado River water during flood time was twenty percent sand and sediment, which he termed "liquid sandpaper."

This is not the case today. Glen Canyon Dam has virtually screened out all of the silt. The crystal waters flowing from the bottom of this dam will continue throughout the three-hundred-

Barrel Cactus on Tonto above Colorado River west

mile distance to Lake Mead unless the muddy Paria and Little Colorado rivers are flowing. This clear water was unheard of in 1701 when Father Kino bestowed the name "Colorado" on the river, reflecting the red tint of the heavily silted water.

It might seem improbable that a single river, no matter how forceful, could have cut so deeply into the past in such a relatively short time—only ten million years to dig into rock almost two billion years old. Uplift has helped. The Grand Canyon region rose to its present elevation as a wide plateau long before the river began its work there. A huge upheaval took place over millions of years, which raised contiguous portions of Utah, Colorado, New Mexico, and Arizona.

This uplift may have actually reversed the Colorado River's direction of flow. Some geologists are studying such a theory, suggesting that the Colorado River above Grand Canyon at one time—some two billion years ago—flowed from what is today Colorado and Utah south and then east into the Rio Grande drainage basin. When the plateau uplift occurred, the river was forced the opposite direction, flowing into what is today Grand Canyon. Interesting as the idea is, it's important to remember that it is still a theory—one that attracts considerable debate.

The Grand Canyon's time frame far exceeds that of humans, who, by the most liberal estimates, appeared on earth only three million years ago. Evidence of higher life in any form, in fact, remains in the upper half of all the canyon's many layers. Primitive fossils appear in the Redwall, with no life at all evident in the Vishnu Schist—green fire hardened to the truth of time.

Harvey Butchart, one of the Grand Canyon's most expert hikers and author of three trail books, tells of the largest amphibian footprints he has seen in the old park area. Located in lower Marble Canyon where the Redwall sinks to river level, the prints are as large as a man's hand. There are distinct impressions along the fore part of the inside edge of the prints, as if there were three toes on that side of the foot. Butchart estimates their age to exceed two hundred million years—rather young when compared with the little sea lilies and tiny stem-fastened animals whose fossils appear in the Redwall at least a hundred and fifty million years earlier.

Floating the Colorado has been described as the experience of a lifetime. Where else to see such hideaways as Vasey's Paradise, Elves Chasm, and Deer Creek Falls; to bounce down Hance Rapid or plunge over Crystal Rapid or Lava Falls, the latter having earned the reputation of being the fastest navigable rapid in the world? Where else to make new friends or get to know oneself? Personalities have a way of rolling out on the river. Where else to get such a sense of history and time?

The Colorado River passes many natural wonders. Some can be seen from the river, others require a hike to remote hideaways. By river or by trail, these secluded and magical areas are bound to inspire awe. Just when all existence seems to be rock and sand, a mystical grotto filled with lush ferns and clear running water appears.

A thick band of stone curves sixty feet overhead. It shoots out of a high cliff and drops to the ground at the crumpled feet of an opposing wall. The stone arc is wide enough to support soil for desert grasses, rabbitbrush, pricklepoppy, yucca—a soft looking but spiny carpet of vegetation—in spite of the sheer canyon walls that block out morning and evening sunlight.

Purling down this canyon and underneath the arch is a narrow stream of clear water, whose stone floor curves just as it reaches the natural

Royal Arch

bridge. Halfway through this canyon passage, the stream runs down a tiered rock shelf into an oblong pool. Mosses wave from the pool's ankle-deep bottom, signaling that the flow is perennial. In another twenty feet, the water falls over a sharp shelf into a tub-sized pool. Two more shelves below that, just beyond a hundred-foot palisade, everything disappears. The bottom drops away with purpose. A hundred feet down and the canyon floor channels the stream toward the Colorado River.

This is Royal Arch, a hideaway in the Grand Canyon. Hideaways come in many shapes and sizes: a spring, a grassy meadow, waterfalls, a sudden valley, a red-patina chasm, a small tree-studded mesa, or an arch. These will embrace an explorer when least expected.

Royal Arch is a surprise. The approach winds for several miles down a flash-flood canyon called Royal Gorge. Scramble up, squeeze through, slide down. Only then do you have clearance to proceed through this boulder-strewn path. About a half-mile before Royal Arch, the stream appears. It arrives, seemingly, by osmosis—actually by a combination of bubbling up from beneath the gravel floor and leaking out of the canyon walls. True to a universal pattern, the thrust of Royal Gorge spoons out its contours

Fern and springs, Kanab Canyon

with tree trunks, silt, an occasional boulder—any tools it can find.

The stream is adorned by delicate plant life. Ferns dangle over miniature stone steps below the undercut. Filmy tamarisk trees drape against the inner wall. Desert grasses sprout softly from diminutive sand dunes. Wildflowers peek out here and there.

Suddenly the right wall rises straight from the water's edge. The left wall is guarded by a huge boulder, which makes a foot-defying slope away from a shallow pool. Slogging down through the charm of the final turns enables one to stand under Royal Arch without realizing it's there. Look up and there it is, a thick stone band in place of sky. Below the arch, where the canyon bottom has dropped away beyond the palisade, Royal Creek continues to the Colorado River. Just before reaching the river, it cuts Elves Chasm.

Elves Chasm is a shy thing. The stream from Royal Gorge trickles down behind a jumbled rock facade and drops into a reflecting pool. Braving cold water, one can swim across this pool and climb up into the chasm itself. Ferns and mosses drape wantonly about the skin-smooth rock cleavage. The place is tactile. Its beauty, the pools and beaches below the chasm,

Elves Chasm

Moss on rock, Serpentine Canyon

can entice a hiker into idling away hours.

One of the Grand's larger hideaways sits below the north rim. A long, lazy bowl cradled above most of the Redwall, Surprise Valley extends for two miles between Deer Creek and Thunder River. It is located on the last mesquite- and sage-dotted shelf before the Colorado River's dispute with the inner gorge.

Along the trail above Surprise Valley, sandy footpaths wind across flat red rock, among juniper and piñon pines, and over the Esplanade. Beyond this Christmas-colored strollway stretches one of the most expansive vistas the canyon contains. The backbone of side canyons above the inner gorge finally disappears as it bends at the end of fifty blue miles toward Diamond Creek.

Deer Creek

Springtime adorns the valley with wildflowers. A wet April can produce a melange of blue and red and at least five different shades of yellow. Three of these yellow shades may appear on the same stem. Descending from the west end of Surprise Valley, the trail arcs over a hearty spring. The noise of wall-gushing water becomes apparent before the ensuing stream is seen feeding Deer Creek.

Deer Creek itself offers a hideaway few have ever visited; this is the lower canyon, cut by the creek just before it drops almost a hundred feet into the Colorado River. The chuckling current accompanies the trail for many yards, then falls with deceptive swiftness. Within only steps, the water disappears, leaving one of the most striking side canyons in the entire complex. Horizontal light and dark brown stripes parallel deeper and deeper through narrow twists and turns that compel one to lean farther and farther over the edge to see if the bottom is visible where the water's sound is vanishing.

Deer Creek Falls is more than eighty feet high, surging through such a twisted trough of rock that the spout cannot be seen from any one place. The hidden waters at the top of the falls seem to wash smoothly through sheer stone sides. At the bottom, the plunging water meets a pool bound for union with the Colorado.

Thunder River announces its presence at the east end of Surprise Valley. As a hiker crosses the valley and exits up the far rise, water can be heard before it becomes visible, particularly in spring when winter snowmelt has charged the water table beneath the rim so profusely that the river spurts straight out of its cave. There is no crossing it this time of year. One must be content to hike down the adjacent trail and cool the feet in a side pool, safely away from the torrential current. Since the river drops two thousand feet in half a mile, these pools are few.

There is a wide rock shelf near the top that can be explored in autumn, along with the cavern from whence Thunder River enters the world. With the water table's winter snowcharge depleted, networks of autumn fern and moss will hang merely moist instead of foam-hidden as in spring runoff. Thunder River is probably the nation's shortest river and the only one that flows into a creek—Tapeats Creek, itself a lengthy hideaway half a mile down the slope.

One of the largest and most popular, yet most Edenic, of hideaways is Havasu Canyon. Three majestic waterfalls—Mooney, Navajo, and Havasu—adorn a two-mile span. Mooney Falls, the highest, drops two hundred feet. The others

Spring feeding Deer Creek

Travertine formation, Mooney Falls

are almost as high. So picturesque is Havasu Falls, that it is also called Bridal Veil Falls.

The word havasu translates literally into "blue water" (*haha* meaning "water," and *vasu* meaning "blue"). The blue color comes from calcium carbonate that precipitates from the water to form travertine. It is travertine that is responsible for a system of large honeycomb-like pools, which the water filters through below the falls before rushing toward the Colorado River.

Canyon bottoms have many special places. Grapevine Canyon, Red Canyon, Hance, and others provide seasonal refuge for wildlife. Exclusive stone holes scooped out of the smooth floor not too many millions of years ago provide water for birds seen flitting about these pools—the canyon wren, the blue-winged teal, warblers, jays, nutcrackers, and (not enough) gnatcatchers.

While these canyons give such gifts freely, even more special hideaways can be found in selected upper reaches—special both in that the spots are intimate and that not many people go to see them. There is one in Red Canyon that would prompt an artist to drag an easel along through the underbrush. The trek requires a climb along the east side of the canyon for a short span. Some sheer pools are lovely but impassable.

Above these impassable pools, there is an inviting grove of cottonwood trees. Just a mile beyond this grove, through a fairly rugged trough of catclaw and boulders and oak saplings, the upper reach of Red Canyon divides. A football field's length to the right, the canyon ends at the bottom of a sheer waterfall—a stained cliff for most of the year—hundreds of feet high.

Only fifty feet up the left fork of this junction, drainage has eaten a deep "V" into a ridge green with vegetation. The left arm of Red Canyon's upper junction stops—or begins—at this sharp angle. The crevice bottom drains down a semicircle of rock shelving about twenty feet above the hiker's head. In a small pool on the floor of the amphitheater, a horsehair worm ten inches long was once spotted. The real attention getter is the way the V-shaped canyon just above the amphitheater has captured a house-sized boulder.

Looming like it might roll out at any moment down the rocky channel below, this huge boulder must have made a marvelous noise when it tumbled from somewhere above, how many hundreds or thousands of years ago. All signs of its initial journey into the crevice are gone. The trees and shrubs it took out have long since grown back. The rock now hangs in suspense,

Havasu Falls

gripped by earthen jaws thirty feet or more above the sharp groove where a springtime creek trickles impassively.

Grapevine Canyon, in keeping with its fellow canyon to the east, also hides a gift in its upstairs closet. The Tonto Trail crosses Grapevine where the canyon divides. The right, or eastern, arm is the more promising because it contains water—once again, a series of enticing pools; tiny chasms etched into the red rock surface over eons of erosion. Face-cooling pools, too small for trout. All the autumn hiker can do is imagine how refreshing the face full of water must be when it's there, unless just after a swift autumn rainstorm. A shower will not do.

The creek that forged these pools also supports a bed of grapevines. Farther up the creek, the springtime blossoms of a distant stand of redbud trees can temporarily fool a hiker into thinking they are peach trees. The upper region just below the Redwall suggests both prehistoric and modern habitation. An unbroken pot was found in a cave here, and the remnants of a mining camp sit on the plateau that edges the Redwall about halfway between Cottonwood and Grapevine canyons.

A few more hideaways among the thousands in the Grand Canyon await hikers on the Grandview Trail before arriving at Cottonwood and Grapevine canyons. This well-known trail tees off of Horseshoe Mesa in a literal sense, with one arm dropping eastward into Hance Canyon and the other dropping westward into Cottonwood. The intersection occurs at the site of another abandoned mining camp. This was known as the Last Chance Copper Mine. The eastern arm tucks down past the abandoned mineshaft. Equipment tantalizes dormantly at the mouth of its cave.

Pause beside a rusty sump pump and imagine the sound, the power, the breakdown of dreams that occurred here just three generations ago. Walk back into the mineshaft, being careful not to hit your head or trip over half-covered rails for the ore car. Coolness will refresh, darkness sooth. Cut marks in the granite will remind how impossible it was to carve the dreamt fortunes from this resource, in spite of award-winning ore. At the Chicago World's Fair, a sample was judged among the richest ever found. Even so, hauling out by muleback proved too expensive.

Not far below, less than halfway down the slope between the mine and Hance Canyon, a pool about the size of a backyard goldfish pond trickles out from beneath a high rock face looking north. Ferns disguise the tuck, hanging like a shaggy green beard around the small mouth with its wet tongue. Simply labeled as "spring" on the map, this pool has been unofficially dubbed the Pharaoh's Bathtub. Hikers are careful not to disturb the delicate moss growth on the pool's shallow bottom.

The most popular creek in the Grand Canyon is the Bright Angel. It cuts the tributary canyon named after it, which has been characterized as the longest, narrowest, and deepest of all side canyons. The creek's sparkling water, Powell reported, suggested the name "Bright Angel" in reciprocation for having named a muddy stream above Glen Canyon the "Dirty Devil." Bright Angel Creek flows past Phantom Ranch, the only inhabited dwelling in the bottom of the national park.

Less than a mile before it reaches this historic site, the Bright Angel's current is reinforced by Phantom Creek. This smaller branch flows into the Bright Angel from the opposite side of the trail, hence requiring wet feet to get there. Not far up the Phantom around two rock bends awaits an idyllic little meadow laced with cottonwood trees. The autumn color these trees emanate above the pastoral stream contributes to the idyllic nature of this place.

Upstream, the Phantom's waters soon be-

Supai sandstone cliffs, Havasu Canyon

come hidden by one of those marvelous rock cleavages. During spring runoff the current may surge; during autumn it tempts with a refreshing gurgle. Here is one of the few places where signs of modern technology might please. There's no passing beyond these smooth rock mounds, at least for the average hiker, without either a hang glider or using some cables anchored by iron rings that surveyors put there years before.

The upper end of Phantom Creek points with frayed fingers to the north rim. An occasional promontory will appear above the creek wall and beckon from the forest primeval thousands of feet above. Climbs are possible to get to the tall pine country.

Five miles upstream from Phantom Creek, the Bright Angel contains another hideaway, perhaps its most famous: Ribbon Falls. To see this one is to understand its name. A thirty-foot, ribbonlike band of water drapes gracefully down an overhanging trough of rock. From where the trail snakes up behind it, the band can be seen to bend, curl, sometimes snap in spray, depending on the caprice of the wind. It will also lull and tranquilize.

This ribbon washes a thirty-foot, cone-shaped pillar of mineral deposits. It is the same travertine that makes the picturesque pools in Havasu Canyon. This pillar appears hollow in places. Its wide foundation in the creekbed below is partially broken away; at the cost of wet feet, one can peek up underneath the crust. The narrow top of the pillar is pitted with rock pockets created by the interaction of falling water and accumulating minerals. Ferns, wildflowers, and other plant life adorn this splashing monument in a botanical mosaic.

An equally charming hideaway is Dripping Springs, whose name befits the manner in which this spring surfaces. A tree-filled draw prepares one for the pastoral setting. The path winds amidst shade and shadows, and at the end of a rather rough approach, a huge rock overhang beckons. Here one can sit beneath the moss-laden roof and watch the water twinkle.

Vasey's Paradise is even more remote than Elves Chasm. In his journal, Powell describes the wall just above the river as "set with a million brilliant gems." As the Powell party approached, they discovered that the gems were made by sunlight flashing on bursting fountains of water.

The main spring spouts white from its russet wall. It drops straight down for about ten feet, then splashes down a steep stone stairway. Foam outlines each rock shelf as it spreads toward a glen of growth below. Shrubs, vines, and several kinds of wildflowers mark this nearly vertical oasis. No wonder Powell called it a paradise.

Drip in cave near Ribbon Falls

Well-known, little-known, some possibly yet unknown, the Grand Canyon's hideaways offer sanctuary from massive stone monoliths. They are the intimacies of the canyon, proving that the largest of crevices can harbor small, delicate life. When gazing at wide vistas from the canyon rims, it may be hard to imagine the nooks and crannies of pools and meadows and arches that nevertheless are present. Such a vast panorama cannot exist without focal points. Investigation reveals that the hideaways are more numerous than first suspected and certainly more lovely.

FROM RIM TO RIVER

Hiking the Bright Angel Trail—a matrix of experiences. Looking across five miles of space to see Bright Angel Canyon cutting into the north rim. Spying a row of yellow deer painted by prehistoric Indians. Weaving dizzily down a steep but not formidable set of switchbacks. Watching the trees of Indian Gardens grow steadily bigger. Hiking the Bright Angel Trail is eventually crossing the "Little Sahara," a mile-long stretch of summertime sweltering sand, which heats feet beside the cool Colorado River. It is enjoying the only trail in the canyon with built-in water stops.

For years the Bright Angel Trail was a toll trail. If one is going to spend the time and effort

Hiker on Beamer Trail

Bright Angel Trail

required to cut a trail down the Grand Canyon, one might as well get something out of it. At least that's the way the Cameron brothers, Ralph and Niles, must have felt when they first engineered this popular corridor trail, along with Pete Berry, Robert Ferguson, and C. H. McClure. They completed the task of widening an old Indian path into something more passable in 1891.

The idea was to haul copper out by mule and it worked for a decade. So successful was it, in fact, that a group of New England businessmen soon bought the Grand Canyon Copper Company and established its headquarters in Montpelier, Vermont. When, in 1901, the bottom fell out of the copper market, the mine went up for sale again. This time it was bought by William Randolph Hearst, who immediately shut the mines and set about promoting a tourist business through the Fred Harvey Corporation.

The Kaibab Trail appears two canyons east of the Bright Angel. It is one of the longest in the canyon, both north and south sections included. The Kaibab is considered by many to be the most scenic in the canyon. Stand at the top, or on one of the switches, and enjoy plummeting canyon walls: horizontal patterns of Kaibab limestone lay like a thin layer of white frosting over

Vishnu Temple from Cape Royal

the thicker Coconino sandstone, which drops vertically onto the reddish slanted shelf of the Supai formation. Tree change is also prominent. Ponderosa pines filtering around sharp Coconino cliffs soon give way to smaller piñon and juniper on the russet Supai shelf.

Cedar Ridge is on this Supai level. At the edge of rolling terrain, the walls of Pipe Creek drop to the demands of a threadlike stream of water. The millions of years required to carve this one side canyon can only be imagined.

The switches down from Cedar Ridge expose the eastern vista—Wotan's Throne, Vishnu Temple, Unkar Rapids. Even if their names and locations were unknown, these features would remain equally as striking. Before curving below O'Neill Butte, the trail razorbacks between both eastern and western vistas: Powell Plateau, a twenty-five-mile stretch to the west; the Desert Palisades, a fifteen-mile stretch to the east.

Around a bend some hand-sized amphibian prints can be found indented in a fallen rock just below the trail. Similar prints can be found throughout the canyon, ranging from insect- to human-sized. This particular series of tracks, sloping up the rock in a solid flow, will be the first specimens many hikers see, however, and will carve a special niche in the memory.

Palisades of the Desert, Jupiter Temple from Cape Royal

*O'Neill Butte
from Yaki Point
on South Kaibab Trail*

How far did this fossil rock fall? Two or three oceans at least were needed to press the soft mud surface this animal stepped across, dragging its tail behind it, into a granite mold. Whatever raindrops began carving O'Neill Butte ten million years ago, would have eroded around the fossil rock until this particular chunk broke off and rolled to its present spot thirty yards below the trail.

Those same forces created Cremation Canyon, which the imprinted rock presently overlooks. If the rock fell down to its present position, then the amphibian creature that made the tracks walked a thousand feet or so above today's spectators, somewhere near the top of O'Neill Butte. Cremation Canyon would have been but a shallow drainage ditch, no doubt a good bit higher than it is today.

Cremation Canyon cuts sharply into the Tonto Plateau, though not as formidably as many. Its walls are scalable at several places, although the Tonto Trail across it will be preferable if one has somewhere to go. Indians claim to have cremated their dead and cast the ashes into this canyon. Interesting how this modern trail parallels a canyon containing some of the oldest known prehistoric carvings.

To leave the Bright Angel and Kaibab trails is to leave the security of people, water stops, emergency phone lines, and the assuredness of knowing where you are. Now it's time for the unimproved and unmaintained trails; this means fewer people, numerous washouts and rock scrambles, water stashes, paying more attention to topographic maps, or traveling with someone who knows the way. There are still a hard-core few who hike these trails as loners. Harvey Butchart emulated the famed mountain men, particularly Bill Williams, by many times doing off-trail and unimproved route hiking without a companion. Most hikers on the unimproved, however, go in pairs; this is big-time hiking.

There are a dozen or so well-known unimproved trails in the Grand Canyon. The four most popular trails run almost alphabetically from west to east: Bass, Hermit, Hance, and Tanner. The first two are on the west side of Grand Canyon Village and the corridor trails (the Bright Angel and the Kaibab), while the remaining two are roughly equidistant from the village on the east side.

The Bass Trail is the only one of these trails that trickles down both rims. Today's North Bass Trail is overgrown and often difficult to find. More than a decade ago, Butchart used such terms as "dim" and "hardly recognizable" for describing parts of it.

The South Bass Trail is more popular. The walk among tall trees is cool and offers an unbroken view of Shinumo Amphitheater across the river. The trail swings out of the Coconino with a sharp left turn through a creekbed. An old fence remains, clinging to a steep slope of Supai formation. The fence stops dutifully at the trail with a wood gatepost, although the gate is no longer there. Just beyond, cliff dwellings are tucked beneath a high vertical overhang. Too small for human habitat, these compartments were probably used as granaries.

Bass was no doubt the most domestic of the Anglo canyon dwellers. At Belrock Tanks, Bass's camp at the river, tools and buckets reveal how a pipe was driven into a rocky crack beneath an overhang to get water. Other signs of settlement include mine shafts, a ferry site for

Across Shinumo Amphitheater from Dutton Point on Powell Plateau

river crossings, and a once-fruitful garden complete with grapevines and peach and apricot trees. Bass also maintained two trams for crossing the river when floods made the ferry crossing dangerous.

The next popular trail moving eastward is named for a man's nickname. This is the Hermit, avenue to the once-popular Hermit Camp and a tram cable, which, incidentally, lowered the only automobile to ever see the Tonto Plateau. The "hermit" of Hermit Trail was Louis Boucher, not really a hermit at all—though riding a mule as white as his beard he may have looked like one. Quiet, to be sure, Boucher was rather sociable. He rescued a few river runners, in fact, and entertained an occasional guest. Hermit Camp was established on the east bank of Hermit Creek, just an hour's walk from the Colorado River. While its abandoned buildings are easily spotted today from Lookout Point, the ruined cabins are still a two-hour walk for most.

Past an upper canyon junction leading to Dripping Springs and the less-popular Boucher Trail (which the hermit built twenty years before the Santa Fe Railroad built the Hermit Trail), the Hermit Trail begins descending through the piñon- and juniper-studded Supai formation.

Two miles down the trail, curving just below Hermit's Rest, an old watering place and a tie bar for animals accompany an ivy-covered shelter along with what must have been an outhouse. This is Santa Maria Spring, constructed in 1913. Today's backpacker can only imagine the pack trains of tourists; for, although this trail remains popular, no mules or horses will be seen on it. The National Park Service ceased maintenance in 1931. It is not unusual to encounter some ice falls in this area in winter, particularly below Santa Maria Spring. Time frozen to test dexterity.

The remaining two trails are named after their builders, Hance and Tanner. John Hance has a colorful reputation, and like Boucher, he rode a white mule to match his flowing white beard. Unlike Boucher, Hance spent many years in the canyon, remaining until his death in 1919, when he was buried in the Pioneer Cemetery.

Homesteading there in 1884, Hance was the first resident of the Grand Canyon. He built the first cabin, at the head of his trail. He also guided the first tourists, including the first woman, to the bottom of the canyon on the Old Hance Trail. After selling his ranch and trail to J. Wilbur Thurber, the stage-line operator, Hance became the first canyon postmaster. In 1897 he

North rim from Hermit Trail

operated the post office of Tourist, Arizona, next to his cabin. In spite of all these firsts, however, Hance fell on hard times.

His tall tales saved him. Winters were severe, as they still can be on the 7,000-foot rim, and Hance would take refuge in another cabin below the rim. During the early years, he was sometimes hungry. After he sold his ranch, trail, and mine interests, Hance was offered permanent residence at the Bright Angel Lodge by the Fred Harvey Company. All he had to do in return was what he did best—entertain tourists with his tall tales.

He once expressed fear that the canyon was being filled up by rocks tourists were throwing into it. He also claimed that an Indian pursuit forced him to attempt to jump the canyon on his horse, Roaney. Roaney didn't quite make the gap, and Hance spun out several versions of how he saved the two of them: by grabbing tree limbs, by jumping off just before they hit bottom, or, perhaps most inventively, by simply reining in and yelling, "whoa!"

Hance fought for Grant during the Civil War, but only after being captured by Yankees while fighting for Lee. He was called "Captain" at the canyon, and for all he endured, it might have been major or colonel or general. Sheer canyon walls and a marvel of wilderness were required to keep John Hance's character intact. New York or Kansas City or Los Angeles would not have done.

There are two Hance Trails, the "old" and the "new." The original trail left the rim at what is now an overlook to Sinking Ship Rock. The first portion of the trail is intact, protected by the steep bowl-like lip of its parent ravine. Footing becomes tricky as the path disappears through the Coconino; then hikers must make their best way down a long talus slope. Once through the Redwall between Sinking Ship Rock and Coronado Butte, it is a pleasant hour's walk to Hance Canyon Campground.

Hance Canyon, oddly enough, does not lead to Hance Rapid. At the mouth of Hance Canyon lurks the hungry Sockdolager Rapid. This rapid does not enjoy the reputation of Hance Rapid but it seems to have frightened the Powell expedition even more. On east around Mineral Canyon, which has an overhang that compels most backpackers to crawl carefully past a sharp drop, Hance Rapid awaits at the termination of Red Canyon, two canyons east.

Red Canyon is topped by a sign that announces the "New Hance Trail." John Hance built this one in 1894 when the old one washed out. Forested shelves adorn the New Hance Trail to the Supai, where it veers east of the Red Canyon hideaway. The trail offers spectacular views; before cracking through the Redwall, an observant hiker can glimpse the lower canyon, that is, Red Canyon itself, through a pair of narrow crevices. The Red Canyon, or New Hance, Trail is more scenic than the Old Hance Trail because it remains high for several miles.

Like the Hance Trail, the Tanner Trail has also been relocated, although not as drastically. The original Tanner Trail came down Cedar Canyon just north of Desert View; of course, none of the Desert View complex was there at the time. Seth Tanner was completing his improvement of an old Indian trail in 1889; the Desert View ranger station was built in 1925, and the watchtower—a Mary Jane Colter marvel—was completed in 1932.

The present Tanner Trail begins at Lipan Point and switches easily down to 75 Mile Canyon saddle. Footing is easy on this popular trail to the saddle, which opens to a spectacular vista. The trail then winds onto a wide island of tree-dotted Supai and slips below Escalante and Cardenas buttes for another mile or two before dropping through the Redwall. In summer, the vermilion Hakatai shale below the Redwall can heat feet. The 1902 Mathes surveying crew had to keep moving so the rocks would not burn their feet through the hobnail soles of their boots. During a wintry storm, a soaking rain below the Redwall can turn to ice and snow above it.

Tanner has an equally colorful reputation. Though a Mormon who "directed many of the Saints" to safe crossings of the Little Colorado riverbed, Tanner was evidently unable to maintain a high moral standard for his trail. It became a haven for everyone from horsethieves to bootleggers.

Before the turn of the century, rumors abounded that John D. Lee had buried several pots of gold along the Tanner. Those who came looking for the gold soon ran the risk of losing

Rainbow over canyon from New Hance Trail

their horses, if not their hides, for the route became handy for horsethieves. Just below the Redwall along the old trail is a large rain pocket, as Butchart describes it, where a sizeable herd of horses could be grazed and watered long enough for brands to be changed. For a number of years the thieves worked between Kanab and Flagstaff, often stealing the very horses they'd sold a few months earlier. According to Butchart, the thieves swam their horses across the river just below Lava Creek (not to be confused with Lava Falls, a hundred miles downstream). A rough trek northward behind Temple and Chuar buttes then intersects the Nankoweap Trail, the other end of the horsethief route.

As if the thievery wasn't enough, someone set up a distillery and began selling bootleg whiskey along the Tanner. During prohibition times, the illegal booze was allegedly sold at the Grand Canyon Village.

Lifelines in dirt, the Grand Canyon's trails. A snowmelt or spring thaw turns crisp bootprints into mud-clinging glop. A slide backward for every two strides upward. Controlled slip-skids going downhill—careful around the curves. Okay when dry.

Avenues of adventure, provided the life-support systems—food, shelter, all-important water—are adequate. How fine the line between exhilarating wilderness experience and disaster.

Pathways to eternity.

To appreciate the Grand Canyon's impact, to better picture the vastness that harbors such intimacy, some perspectives must be taken. A time frame, for instance, helps communicate the meaning of rock layers. With fossils of both plant and animal life, each of the nine major rock layers tells how the region developed during eras between engulfing oceans. These eras varied from lifeless, to a time of lush tropical forests eventually covered by a barren desert, to the alpine forest we see today.

The time frame points halfway to the beginnings of the earth. About five billion years ago we were a mass of gas. Four billion years ago solid matter had appeared. Three billion years ago the rock layer was formed that now channels the Colorado River through the bottom of the Grand Canyon. This is the Vishnu Schist, among the oldest exposed rock in the world.

The Vishnu Schist has impressive battle scars. It was made by fire and cooled to a crust. The igneous shell was then cracked open by interior movement, expanding and contracting. Molten granite ran into the cracks to make the striking pink and greenish veins visible today. The Vishnu Schist contains no fossils. It is older than life. The subsequent rock layers have been made by a series of seas and intervening forests and deserts with varying climatic conditions depositing layer upon layer of progressing life forms.

Some of the most interesting aspects of the entire natural lamination process are found near the top—the most recent deposits. The present rimming layer of the Grand Canyon—the Kaibab limestone—was not always the top layer. With the time frame still hovering between two and three hundred million years ago, the Coconino layer, that line of tall whitish-brown cliffs a few hundred feet below the top, was deposited. This was made, like the others, by a slow sea; this particular sea, however, left behind its receding waters a thick desert, which millions of years of winds rolled and rippled into sand dunes. Within the next hundred million years, the Toroweap layer was deposited, and on top of that the Kaibab, where an alpine forest now grows. Today the Toroweap is seen as a series of slopes sandwiched between the more prominent strata of Coconino below the Kaibab on top.

In time—still eons before human life—after the deposit of the Kaibab, another layer was deposited above it, and another layer above that, for still more oceans washed over and continued to leave their sediments. These were not layers of rocks; oceans do not deposit rocks. Each sediment layer required time and weight before it would be pressured into becoming a rock formation. Thus, the Coconino deposit remained an underground desert long after it was entombed beneath the Toroweap and Kaibab, becoming a band of rock only gradually, as many additional layers of sediment were piled on top.

When this sedimentary action finally stopped, the Kaibab lay ten thousand feet underground. More importantly, like the Coconino, the Kaibab layer—subject to time and pressure—was transformed eventually into the latest layer of rock.

At this point in time, rain began washing away whatever deposits had not become sufficiently hard enough to resist erosion. This meant everything down to the Kaibab, where the erosion was arrested and could only cut into nooks and crannies—the beginnings of the Grand

Snag near Yavapai Point

Canyon, which started a scant ten million years ago.

A conspicuous bluff just south of Grand Canyon village stands in testimony and a kind of defiance of the process. This is Red Bluff, or Tusayan Mountain, which somehow withstood enough of the eroding action to remain perched several hundred feet above the surrounding plateau. It is a solitary thing, standing above gently rolling terrain like a huge earthen submarine to be seen a hundred miles away on a clear day. Prehistoric Indians found the bluff attractive, possibly a shrine.

Amidst the hideaways and along the trails of Grand Canyon, plants and animals thrive from rim to inner recesses. Archaeological finds suggest that a more accommodating environment existed during the last several thousand years than current semiarid conditions might indicate, and canyon life reveals a remarkable ability to adapt to changing conditions. The experienced canyoneer discovers that while the rock pattern remains permanent, the Grand Canyon is at the same time a record of change. The plant life teems and thrives; a diminutive yet persistent gnawing at exposed surfaces keeps the canyon alive.

The cycle works. A decayed tree enriches soil for new growth. Dead trees also provide food and habitat for bugs and insects, mice, chipmunks, and squirrels along with several types of birds. Larger animals monitor the process.

A rock pocket mouse can nestle in his winter home beneath a fallen tree, safe from hawks and eagles and turkey vultures. Yet a bear could tear into the tree in search of a midnight snack; if he does not capture the mouse itself, he will at least roust the rodent for a nearby owl or coyote.

The observant hiker can witness this life process: pinecones dropping from a piñon tree accompanied by the flick of a squirrel tail; the crash of deer dashing up a sage-filled ravine; the swoop of a raven's wing; the flash of a spooked rainbow trout or the rarer golden trout, which appears at first as a wavering shadow; the glint of a gray-winged goshawk on its blinding flat dive for songbirds among crouching mesquite and juniper trees. The most common sign of coyote will be a pile of scat prudently deposited atop a conspicuous rock, frequently in the middle of the trail. This is canyon life: real though momentary, essential though capricious as critterprints across spring morning snowfilm.

Each animal, small and large, stalking the canyon's surface or burrowed into its depths, is a

Saddle Canyon

center of life. Each exhibits intriguing, but not always successful, patterns of survival. The kangaroo rat, for instance, manufactures all the water it ever needs through its food digestion. With this internal hydro system, it can go through life without taking a drink. The grasshopper mouse is an almost equally avid teetotaler; its fare of insects and an occasional fellow mouse provide much of the water this rodent requires. The most innovative of canyon rodents may be the antelope ground squirrel. When things get too hot for this little chap, he simply salivates on his chest fur, creating instant evaporative cooling.

The rich evergreen forests of the canyon rims host two of the most distinctive squirrels in the world, the Abert and the Kaibab. Both squirrels exhibit tufts of hair shooting out the tips of their ears, as if they'd just heard something shocking. The Abert squirrel is by far the more common, ranging southward beyond the massive Coconino National Forest. Its reddish back or the flash of its white belly amidst otherwise bluish-gray fur will distinguish this squirrel from its north rim cousin.

Along the river, and up who knows how many side canyons, the ringtail cat may appear.

Chances are slim that a ringtail will be seen in years of hiking, because they are almost totally nocturnal. Their prints, however, can sometimes be spotted in sandy stretches of trail and riverbank.

Three of the larger, and to some the most alluring, forms of wildlife in the canyon are the bear, bighorn sheep, and deer. Bear sightings are few for several reasons. Only the shy black bear inhabits the canyon's forested regions anymore and its numbers are now few and far between. Also, since this bear is largely nocturnal, a person could hike a lifetime without seeing one. During winter they do not really hibernate; their body temperature remains close to normal. The male may venture forth during warm spells, but the female generally stays in her separate den all winter long to nurse the family. Watch for big five-toed tracks accompanied by broken bush twigs, an old log or a standing dead tree that's been clawed open, or undigested juniper berries in a fresh scat deposit.

Bighorn sheep have been referred to as the ghosts of the Grand Canyon; they can appear and disappear before your eyes. A herd of bighorn reportedly frequents the area between the Kaibab and Bright Angel trails, the two most popular trails in the park. Along these two busiest of canyon trails, however, reports of bighorn sightings are rare.

For the fortunate few, a bighorn may appear—one or two, maybe the entire herd. They are the color of the upper canyon rock, so will be noticed probably by moving shadows or changing shapes. It's not at all unrealistic to imagine a majestic buff-colored ram, statue still, peering stoically from an overhang along the Redwall or Coconino, watching antlike human figures trek across the Tonto Plateau or the southern Esplanade. A slight shift of curled horns would betray an even slighter head movement. Its small mouth may flutter for a moment, the upper lip curling back to reveal graze-worn teeth. How many bighorn sheep have watched oblivious hikers in the canyon?

The most prolific of the larger canyon creatures are the mule deer. They get their name not because they're stubborn, although they do sometimes seem stupid, but because of their large ears, which they will fan at the slightest sound. Unlike the whitetail, which thrives next to people but runs long distances when flushed, mule deer prefer to remain farther from civilization but will run only a short distance when spooked.

Mule deer have now become so accustomed to sharing the Grand Canyon with human bipeds that they may stand quite close to people and watch them pass, or merely dash around a ravine only to be flushed fifteen minutes later by the same hikers.

Humans are the newcomers. The hundreds of cliff dwellings extant in the Grand Canyon suggest that thousands may have inhabited the area. Petroglyphs and paintings announce early human residence.

In the canyon itself, however, no footprints. Where have they gone? Some like to think they never were—to pretend the entire vast land of America was vacant so that Anglos displaced no one to occupy it. But the Grand Canyon was indeed inhabited. Butchart has remarked how the field of wild cane along the east side of Deer Creek suggests an agricultural impulse among dwellers of that isolated locale. Similarly attractive settings exist at several other spots along the Colorado River.

Only eight thousand years ago, less than a penny's worth of the canyon's ten million years, prehistoric Indians came to the Colorado Plateau. These Indians hunted and gathered. Hence they roamed, depending upon game populations and seasonal growth patterns for subsistence. The

Mule deer, Little Nankoweap Delta

canyon rims and surrounding high desert regions must have been bountiful, at least enough to support these small kin-related groups of people. The first gatherers were "desert culture" people, the ones who visited the canyon's inner recesses but did not reside there.

Anthropologists identify the Anasazi as the first to permanently inhabit the canyon itself, although like the desert culture people, some of the Anasazi also lived on the rims. Hundreds of sites have been found in and around the canyon, with concentrations south of Nankoweap and near the bend about Cape Royal and Wotan's Throne. Since they knew how to farm, the Anasazi did not roam as widely or as often as the prior desert culture people. They became prosperous, thriving until A.D. 1200 when they disappeared.

Simultaneous with the Anasazi lived the Cohonina. These people, from whom we get the modern name "Coconino," established themselves southwest of the Grand Canyon. They traded with the Anasazi, farmed as well as hunted and gathered, and thrived within the same time frame, achieving their greatest prosperity between A.D. 700 and 1000. Whatever forces drove the Anasazi away from their Grand Canyon homes, seem to have driven the Cohonina into the beautiful blue-watered Havasu Canyon.

Cliff dwellings above Nankoweap Delta

Petroglyphs, Cataract Canyon

The rocks, the animals, even early humans grip time dimensions that can be counted. Years number into billions for rock, millions for animals, at least thousands for humans. One of the most dramatic features of canyon perspectives, however, cannot be counted, although it continually captures the attention of scientist, hiker, and artist. These are the cloud patterns.

It has often been noted that the canyon has moods and seems to change continuously throughout any given day. These moods are the influence of sunlight and clouds. Clouds echo the impulse of intimacy. They often mimic the contour below them. They will sweep upwards along a bluff, spiral down a palisade, or hang like a lumpy carpet to soak a usually dusty mesa top.

Comanche Point from Tanner Trail

They will cut the top off Battleship Rock and the bottom out from under Sinking Ship Rock.

Clouds in the Grand Canyon form a single purple face that approves and disapproves simultaneously of the wary, watching hiker; or they can float like separate puffs of blanched cotton candy, casting curled shadows on a sun-specked talus slope. These misty mid-regions of light and shadow reveal perhaps more than any other single phenomenon the canyon's caprice. The clouds can coagulate into an opaque screen, hiding the next bend in the trail, then part their vestment to let a hiker see the last few hours' progress, or the next few. They can open around the sun and tint their puffy framework with a renaissance glow; then squeeze together so thick as to lure a person to walk across them. And they can hide completely away for days.

The Grand Canyon will prompt praise, solidify friendships, foster admiration. It can become a man's mistress, a woman's lover. The place is a paradox. It is constant, yet constantly changing. It is vast and abstruse, yet acutely specific. It is older than life, yet harbors unique life forms from fish to flowers. It will feed and shelter one man, yet kill another. And it does each of these things all at the same time.

From river to rim, from rim to river. And everything in between. That's what it's all about. Experiencing the intimacy of the Grand Canyon requires more than a look, more even than a book of description. It requires understanding and, perhaps more importantly, caring. Nowhere else can a river like the Colorado or a canyon like the Grand be found. We cannot divorce either from political actions. The public must be not only informed but must also aspire to preserve the place.

Nature: common denominator of the world. The Grand Canyon reduces this denominator to a perfect exponent. The natural wonder is a product of whatever power is applied to it. The Grand Canyon has been able to heal, help, hurt, kill, teach, provide, enrich, impoverish, reduce, depress, or inspire depending on how it is experienced. Here one can truly sense the intimate.

Winter vista from Bass Trailhead

I stand on the brink of gaping space.
Below me, the land falls away
into a labyrinth of gorges, ravines, and terraces,
with endless variations of pattern and color.
Miles away, the North Rim
at last confines the great expanse.
Spellbound, I cannot turn away.

MARK JEFFERSON

View from Yaki Point

DOWLING GRAY CAMPBELL is an assistant professor of English at Northern Arizona University. He first hiked the Grand Canyon ten years ago, and as he spent more time there, began to study it. Although he has hiked in several other areas in the Southwest, the Grand Canyon remains his special love: "I admired the canyon when I hiked it in ignorance; as I get to know it even better, I cherish it even more." An experienced canoer and kayaker, Campbell also enjoys floating through the canyon.

MARK JEFFERSON has been hiking and photographing the Grand Canyon for the past ten years. He has worked seasonally at national parks and for the U.S. Forest Service since 1970 when he first came west. A hiker, biker, and mountain climber, Jefferson has traveled extensively in the North Cascades, the Sierra Nevada, and the Rocky Mountains in addition to his many adventures in Grand Canyon. During a fifty-four-day expedition through the canyon in 1979, Jefferson took many of the photographs included in this book. He currently lives in Flagstaff where he continues to photograph the natural surroundings.